DISCOVER

BUGS

Contents

Bug World

Bugs are creepy, crawly creatures that live in the garden, under stones, and even in your house. Commonly called insects, bugs are small, six-legged animals. There are over a million species or types of insects – much more than all the animal and plant types put together!

■ The wings of the peacock butterfly are reddish-brown on top and dark brown to black underneath. They have special marks on the wings, which look like false eyes

Living zones

Look around anywhere and you are sure to find a bug. Insects can live almost anywhere on Earth – from hot tropical jungles to snow-capped mountains and scorching deserts. They can be found in caves and burrows deep in the ground, or flying high in the sky. Some insects can even live on an animal's body, or inside it!

Tasty bite

Most insects feed on plants. But bugs are usually unfussy about food and can eat almost anything. They are known to feed on fabrics, plaster, cork, face powder, other living things, and even toothpaste!

■ A dragonfly has four large wings that look like fine gauze. As it flies through the air, it holds its legs together to form a basket in which other insects are caught. The dragonfly can eat while flying

Secret of success

Bugs appeared on Earth long before humans. The secret of their ability to survive in just about any conditions lies in their small size, tough outer skeleton and adaptability. Bugs are not choosy about the places they live in or the things they eat. Bugs also have short lives. They quickly become adults and give birth to a large number of babies – each of them better survivors than their parents.

FACT FILE

Smallest
Dwarf beetle; 0.01 inches
Largest
Atlas moth; it has a wingspan of about 9.8 inches (25 cm)
Heaviest
Goliath beetle; weighs up to 3.4 ounces (96.4 g)
Longest
Stick insect; females grow over 14.2 inches (36 cm) in length

■ The black or black-and-orange burying beetles look out for dead mice and other small animals. They bury these animals so they can feed on them

INTERESTING FACT!

Most insects are less than 0.24 inches (6 mm) long. The smallest ones include hairy-winged dwarf beetles. They can easily crawl through the eye of a needle, and are barely visible to the human eye!

Bugging us

We are constantly at war with insects. They annoy us, bite us, infect us with diseases, eat our food, and damage our property. But not all insects are harmful. A lot of them are of great value to us. Some help in pollination, while others serve as food for fish, birds and many other animals. In fact, life on Earth may not exist if all the insects were to disappear!

■ Despite their names, velvet ants are actually a species of wasp. The female velvet ant does not have any wings

Inside Story

Although they come in various shapes, sizes and colors, all bugs have a common body structure. Their body is divided into three main parts – head, thorax and abdomen. All bugs have six legs, arranged in three pairs. They also have a pair of antennae and a tough, shell-like outer covering. Some bugs even have wings.

■ Like with all other bugs, the exoskeleton of a cockroach does not grow as it gets older. Hence, the exoskeleton becomes too tight and needs to be shed. The bug forms a new suit of armour underneath before it crawls out of the old suit

A Madagascar hissing cockroach

Abdomen

A bug's abdomen contains its organs, which are very different from a human being's. Air enters the insect through a few pores in the exoskeleton. These pores are called spiracles. Oxygen is distributed to all areas of the body through breathing tubes. In humans, blood flows through special tubes called blood vessels. In bugs, though, blood flows throughout the body cavity.

Armor suit

Bugs have a shell-like outer covering over their soft bodies. This outer covering is called the exoskeleton. It is usually light and strong, and serves as a suit of armor that protects the bug. The muscles of the bug are attached to the inside wall of the exoskeleton.

INTERESTING FACT!

When insects walk, they usually move the middle leg on one side, with the front and hind legs on the opposite side. In this way, they are always firmly supported – like a three-legged stool.

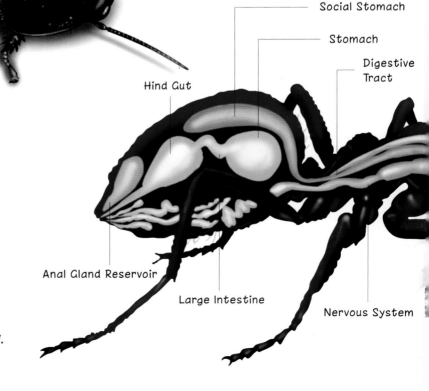

Social Stomach

Stomach

Digestive Tract

Hind Gut

Anal Gland Reservoir

Large Intestine

Nervous System

FACT FILE

Fastest-flying insect
Dragonfly; 59 mph
Longest flight
Butterflies and locusts can fly continuously for well over 100 miles. Tiny fruit flies can fly for more than five hours
Shortest flight
Honeybees can fly only for 15 minutes at a time
Wing speed
Large-winged butterflies beat their wings 4 to 20 times per second; houseflies, about 200 times; and some midges about 1,000 times per second
Fastest-moving insect
Cockroach; 3.35 mph

■ insects that chew have powerful grinding jaws called mandibles. The jaws work sideways, not up and down as in humans. The jaws are also modified for sucking

Heady matter

A bug's head includes mouthparts, eyes and the antennae. The mouth has special structures for feeding, which allow the bug to chew or suck. Most adult insects have two enlarged eyes, with a pair of antennae between them. They use these antennae to smell, taste and even hear.

Brain

Eye

Mandible Gland Reservoir

■ Bugs have compound eyes. While humans have just one lens, insects can have thousands of separate lenses. These combine to form a complete picture of what an insect sees

Midzone

The thorax is the middle section of a bug's body. It supports the three pairs of legs and the wings, if present. Bugs can use their legs for running, grasping, digging or swimming.

Changing Times

Nearly every insect starts life as an egg. After hatching, the insect begins to grow and develops into an adult. During this process, most insects go through a series of amazing changes in form. The entire cycle – from egg to adult – takes only a few days for some species, and as long as 17 years for others.

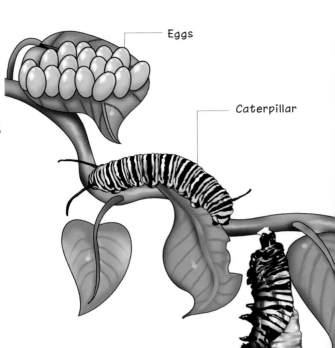

Eggs

Caterpillar

Caterpillar entering pupal stage

Growing up

After an egg hatches, it follows one of three patterns of growth and development, depending on its type. The simplest cycle occurs in a few kinds like silverfish and springtails. When the eggs of these insects hatch, the young ones look exactly like their parents, only smaller. These are called nymphs.

■ This is a trilobite larva, a female bug that grows to maturity while retaining juvenile or larval form

Changing form

Other insects have a far different pattern of growth and development. The young look different from their parents and are called larvae. They change in form as they develop into adults. This change is called metamorphosis.

■ Cicadas plant their eggs in tree branches. On hatching, the nymphs fall to the ground and scurry into the soil, settling near the tree roots. They feed on the sap for 7 years. As they grow larger they moult their exoskeleton - revealing a newly formed one underneath

Types of metamorphosis

There are two kinds of metamorphosis. In incomplete metamorphosis, the nymphal stages look like the adult except that they don't have wings. The nymphs may also be a different color than the adults. In complete metamorphosis, on the other hand, young bugs do not look at all like the adults. The nymphs often live in different habitats, and feed on different things.

Adult butterfly

Adult butterfly coming out of pupa

Pupa about to open

■ After a larva completes its growth, it stops eating and spins a cocoon – a protective covering – around its body. It then becomes a pupa. Inside the covering, it is broken down and re-formed into adult organs. After the change is complete, the pupal covering cracks open and the adult flies out

INTERESTING FACT!

A pair of houseflies could produce millions of babies, if all of them lived! Attacks by parasites, predators, lack of food supply, and other factors prevent many of them from surviving.

Eggs of all shapes

Insect eggs have a variety of shapes and colour patterns, but most are oval or round and are pale- or cream-colored. Insects lay their eggs singly or in batches. They usually lay them on or near food, which the young eat after they hatch.

■ The cockroach's egg case is the size and shape of a baked bean. It can contain from 10 to 20 eggs

Know Your Bugs

Not all small animals that crawl are bugs. A spider is not an insect, and neither is a centipede. In fact, only those crawling creatures that have six legs and a body divided into three parts are called insects.

Caught in a web

Spiders differ from bugs in many ways. While spiders have eight legs, bugs have six. A spider's body is divided into only two main parts, whereas a bug has three parts. Most bugs have wings and antennae, but spiders do not.

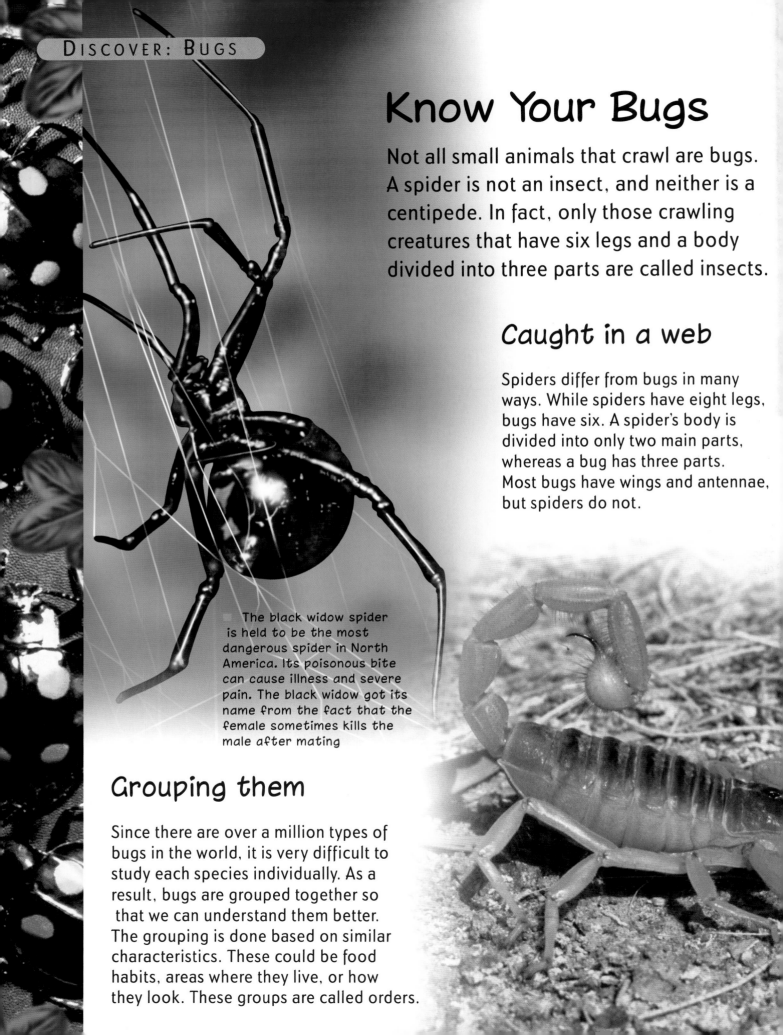

The black widow spider is held to be the most dangerous spider in North America. Its poisonous bite can cause illness and severe pain. The black widow got its name from the fact that the female sometimes kills the male after mating

Grouping them

Since there are over a million types of bugs in the world, it is very difficult to study each species individually. As a result, bugs are grouped together so that we can understand them better. The grouping is done based on similar characteristics. These could be food habits, areas where they live, or how they look. These groups are called orders.

FACT FILE

Life span
Tarantula
Can live up to 30 years
Queen termite
Known to live up to 50 years
Locust
Up to 17 years
Wood beetle
40 years
Mayfly
Just a few hours or one day

■ Although both centipedes and millipedes look similar, they are very different. Centipedes, like this giant desert centipede, can grow up to 20 cm in length, while millipedes are not longer than 10 cm. Most centipedes are venomous, while millipedes roll into a ball when threatened

INTERESTING FACT!

Centipedes and millipedes are not bugs. They have narrow bodies divided into segments. Each section has one or two pairs of legs. Centipedes can have 15 to 175 pairs of legs, while millipedes can have up to 380.

Some disagreement

Entomologists, or people who study bugs, do not agree on the number of orders that exist. Some may consider a certain group of bugs as a single order, but others might regard them as two or more orders. For this reason, some say that there are more than 30 orders, and others list fewer than 25.

■ Scorpions have a poisonous sting at the end of their tails. In some species this sting is capable of killing a human

Naming game

The orders are arranged according to how bugs have developed over millions of years. Since most orders are based on similar features, the name of the order tells us about a particular feature. The feature is usually given at the end of the name as a suffix: the suffix -ura means tail; -ptera, wings; and aptera, wingless.

Bug Senses

Insects depend on their senses of touch, hearing, smell, sight and taste to find their way home, locate food, and protect themselves. While bugs have several special sense organs, the most crucial are the antennae. The sensory deprivation caused by removing an insect's antennae renders individuals of many species types helpless.

■ Some kinds of bugs – including ants, bees and wasps – have taste organs on their antennae. They touch the food with their antennae, and eat it only if they like the taste. Other bugs – including butterflies, some moths and flies and honeybees – taste with their feet!

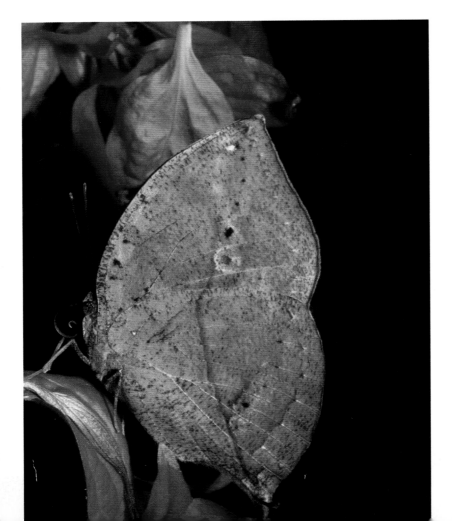

Many lenses

Most bugs have two large compound eyes on their head. While humans have just one lens in their eyes that enables them to focus on objects, bugs have many lenses. Each eye is made up of tiny, six-sided lenses that fit together like a honeycomb.

Smelly factor

A bug's antennae also help it to smell things. It uses its sense of smell to look for food, find its way about, and locate places to lay eggs. Ants and bees recognize other members of their colony by their odor.

■ Bugs like the dragonfly can only see a short distance. Objects more than one metre away appear as a blur to them, but they can see broad movements, as well as recognize colors. Bugs have no eyelids and so their eyes are always open

Touchy creatures

Bugs have excellent sensory perception. They sense the air around them with the hairs and spines that cover their body and antennae. Bugs can even feel a change in the air around them. That is why no matter how carefully you move your hand towards a fly, it will always fly away!

■ Bristles, or fine hairs, on the antennae and the legs help bugs to hear, smell, taste and even feel objects!

■ A bug's ears can be located almost anywhere on the body, but never in the head. For instance, the narrow-beaked katydid has ears on its legs!

INTERESTING FACT!
Bugs do not have real voices. Many of them rub body parts against each other to make sounds. Crickets rub their legs together to make chirping sounds, while bees make a humming noise by flapping their wings rapidly.

Hear a whisper

Most bugs can hear sounds that are either too soft or too high pitched for humans. But only a few types of bugs have true ears. Others hear with the delicate hairs on their antennae and body.

Attack and Defence

A bug's life is filled with dangers. It may be eaten by other bugs, birds or animals. Cold weather may kill it, or a dry spell may kill the plants it eats. People are also a threat. Hence, to fight for survival, bugs have developed special means of defense.

Scooting away

Bugs have many defense mechanisms. The most common is to escape by quickly flying, leaping, or scampering away. Some caterpillars and beetles play dead, or adopt threatening postures to frighten the enemy. They also adopt special poses to attack and kill other bugs.

■ The mantis - also called the 'praying mantis' - holds its front legs as if it were praying. It uses its arm-like forelegs to grasp and capture its prey. The mantis is often missed by both its prey and predator because of its excellent camouflage

Weapons of war

Most bugs have weapons with which to deter enemies: bees, wasps and some ants have poisonous stings; certain ants, horseflies and other bugs can pinch with their powerful jaws; caterpillars often have hollow body hairs filled with poison, which break at the slightest touch, releasing the poison; stinkbugs, lacewings and carrion beetles give off foul odors; some butterflies, moths and other bugs are also protected simply because they taste bad to their predators!

■ Male stag beetles have oddly enlarged jaws. They resemble the horns of a male deer and can be as long as the body of the insect. Male stag beetles use these horns against each other in battles for mating rights

Many spider species eat other spiders. Most female spiders are larger and stronger than male spiders, and occasionally eat the males

Mimics for life

Some bugs are great mimics – that is, they resemble other bugs. This often protects weaker bugs if they look like stronger bugs. To illustrate, because a viceroy butterfly resembles the monarch butterfly, birds leave it alone, because the monarch tastes unpleasant to them.

Coloring camouflage

Some bugs also escape their enemies because either their color or form blends with the surroundings. This is called camouflaging. When resting on tree trunks, many moths look like bark or bird droppings. Stick bugs and some caterpillars resemble twigs.

Butterflies are experts at camouflaging. When a leaf butterfly folds its wings, it looks like a dead leaf

Bees and Wasps

Some groups of bugs stay in huge colonies. They are called social bugs. Termites, ants, bees and wasps are all social bugs. These colonies are highly organized and hierarchical.

All in a family

Social bugs live in communities wherein each member depends upon the other. Those living together are often part of the same family. For example, the 60,000 to 80,000 bees in a hive are all born from one queen. So are the millions of termites that may make up a termite colony.

■ A hornet is a kind of wasp that lives in large nests that are shaped like an upside-down pear. These usually hang from branches or leaves

■ Most social wasps make nests of paper. The female produces the paper by chewing up plant fibers or old wood. The paper is spread in thin layers to make cells where eggs are laid

Shared work

Each member of a colony does the work given to it. The queen's job is to lay eggs. The adults in the colony, called workers, feed and care for the young. Termites have both male and female workers, though all the workers among ants, bees and wasps are females.

FACT FILE

For one pound of honey,
bees fly over 55,000 miles
(88,514 km)
An average worker bee
makes 1/12 of a teaspoon of
honey in her lifetime
Honey bees fly at
about 15 mph (24 kmph)
An ant can carry
50 times its own weight

Male zone

Males are found in a colony
of social bugs only for limited
periods of time. The males' only
job is to mate with the queen,
after which they die. In bee
colonies, the males are called
drones, while in termite colonies
they are the kings!

■ Bees eat
only nectar.
Wasps can feed
on other bugs
and human
food as well

INTERESTING FACT!

Social bugs communicate
with one another with the
use of sound, touch and
scent. Honeybees use a form
of dance to tell other
members of the hive the
direction and distance of
where food is to be found.

Different tasks

Each colony member performs
a specialized task. Nurses look
after the young and soldiers
defend the colony from attacks
by enemies. Some workers
search for food, while others
enlarge and clean the nest.

■ Cuckoo bees invade
the nests of bumblebees
and lay eggs there. The
bumblebees raise the
cuckoos' young as their own

Ants and Termites

Ants are among the most successful social bugs. While they may look small and simple, they actually have complex behavioral patterns. The division of work in these colonies, as well as the means to get food, is a highly regimented operation.

Special mounds

Termites construct extremely large and elaborate mounds to house their colonies. These mounds take various forms and are as hard as concrete. On the inside, mounds may have chimneys, a nursery, waste-disposal chambers and a special cell for the queen.

■ The inside of a termite mound is divided into many chambers and galleries. In the center is a closed cell, where the queen dwells

■ The soldier termites are wingless and blind. They are larger in build than the workers, with a huge head, powerful jaws and strong legs

Up in arms

Army ants march across huge distances on land and eat other bugs. A single parade of army ants looks so formidable that even bigger creatures are intimidated. Due to their sheer number, army ants can also attack mice and lizards. If the prey is unable to escape quickly, the ants can overwhelm it by swarming all over it.

■ Leafcutter ants continually collect leaves, which they cut into tiny pieces for easier carrying

FACT FILE

Termite mounds can be
as high as 20 ft. (6m)
Largest ant
over 1 inch (2.5 cm) long
Smallest ant
about .04 in. (0.1 cm) long
Queen ant
lives 10-20 years; workers,
1-5 years; while male ants
survive for just a few months

Slave drivers

Certain kinds of ants keep aphids, caterpillars or other bugs, which they "milk" for food. Many ants raid other ants' nests and carry off the young, which they bring up as slaves.

■ Weaver ants build nests in trees by attaching leaves together. Bridges of workers first pull in the leaves. These leaves are then sewed up by pressing silk-producing larvae against them

INTERESTING FACT!

Ants "talk" to one another by giving off chemicals called pheromones. An ant may lay a scent trail from a newly discovered food supply to its nest. The other workers then follow the trail to the food.

Self-made or thieves

Ants have different ways of gathering food. Harvester ants collect seeds, which are stored in their nests. Thief ants live by stealing food from other ants. Some other species, such as leafcutter ants, actually grow their own food. They cultivate tiny mushroom gardens in their nests!

Winged Wonders

Butterflies are among the most elegant and beautifully marked of all bugs. They have delicate and, often, very colorful wings. Butterflies and moths belong to the same order of winged bugs. They are the only bugs to have scales on their wings.

■ Most butterflies rest with their wings held upright over their bodies. Moths, however, rest with their wings spread out flat

Moth vs butterfly

Although grouped together, moths are not considered as beautiful as butterflies. Moths have plump, furry bodies, while butterflies are slender. Moths also do not have knobs on their antennae like butterflies do. Moreover, while butterflies fly during the day, moths prefer nights.

Before take-off

Butterflies and moths cannot fly if their body temperature is less than 86° F. If the temperature is low, they need to warm up. The bugs either bask in the sun or shake their wings to build up heat.

■ Butterflies attract each other with the colorful patterns on their wings. After mating, the female begins laying eggs within a few hours, but the male dies

Hungry caterpillar

Butterflies and moths undergo a complete change while going through four different life stages. They start life as an egg. The larva or caterpillar hatches from the egg and feeds on leaves or flowers. As it grows, the caterpillar loses its outer skin – in other words, it molts many times.

■ The Heliconid butterfly is also known as the ˝passion flower˝ butterfly. It feeds on the poisonous leaves of the passion-flower. This makes it inedible for other animals

Resting stage

After reaching its full size, the caterpillar turns into a pupa. The pupa is motionless, which is why this is often called the "resting" stage. The adult butterfly is slowly formed within the shell. This stage can last from a few days to over a year.

■ Satyrid butterflies, also called wood nymphs, fly at low heights and in a zigzag manner. On sensing danger, the butterflies stay motionless with closed wings. If the danger continues, they fly away

INTERESTING FACT!
In addition to color and shape, the fragrance of flowers is what really draws butterflies to a garden. Flowers with the strongest perfume are most appealing to a butterfly's sensitive sense of smell.

Along Came a Spider

One of the most common crawling creatures on earth is the spider. But, contrary to popular knowledge, spiders are not bugs. Rather, they belong to a completely different group of creatures, called arachnids. Scorpions also belong to this group.

Living zones

Like bugs, spiders too can live just about anywhere. Spiders are found in fields, woods, swamps, caves and deserts. Spiders help people by eating harmful bugs. They eat grasshoppers and locusts, which destroy crops, and flies and mosquitoes, which carry diseases.

■ A spider never gets caught in its own web. The spider walks across the web, holding on to the silk lines with a special hooked claw on each foot

■ Most spiders enclose their eggs in a sac. The egg sac is a bag made of a special kind of silk. Some spiders hang their sac in a web. Others attach it to leaves or plants. Still others carry it with them. Spiderlings hatch inside the egg sac

Spot the difference

The difference between bugs and spiders can be seen from their body structure. Spiders have four pairs of legs and have only two body segments - a fused head and thorax, and an abdomen.

Spinning magic

Spiders produce silk for their web through special glands. The web is spun through short, finger-like organs called spinnerets, which are attached to the abdomen. A spider can have two, four, or six spinnerets. The tip of a spinneret is covered with tubes, through which liquid silk flows from the glands. The silk later hardens into a thread.

Web of death

Spiders love to feed on bugs and spin webs to catch them. Even bugs that are larger and stronger than spiders cannot escape from the threads of a spider's web.

■ Hunting spiders have good eyesight at short distances. Web-building spiders, on the other hand, have poor eyesight. Their eyes are used for detecting changes in light

INTERESTING FACT!
More than 150 spiders were used in the movie "Spider-Man." They were specially picked for the role. Those who made it to the big screen had the best spider behaviour!

■ Orb weavers spin the most beautiful webs. Many orb weavers spin a new web every night. And it takes them just about an hour to do so. These weavers often wrap their victims in sheets, just like mummies

Knights in Shining Armor

Beetles are the toughest looking bugs around. Unlike other bugs, adult beetles have a pair of special front wings called elytra. They form a leathery cover, protecting the beetle's body. Beetles are called the 'armored tanks' of the insect world, because of their hard wings and shell-like exoskeleton.

Amazing variety

Beetles live everywhere on Earth except in the oceans. They vary greatly in shape, color and size. Some, such as click beetles and fireflies, are long and slender. Others, including ladybugs, are round. Most beetles are brown, black or dark red in color though some can have bright, shiny rainbow colors.

■ Fungus beetles feed on spores of fungi. They also mess up the areas they live with their waste and cast skins

■ The mouths of adult weevils are at the tip of a long snout, which is used to bore into fruits, seeds and other plant parts. The larvae have no legs and feed on the inside of fruits and nuts and are called borers. Weevils are known for destroying crops

Legs for work

Like their shape and color, the legs of a beetle also vary. Each of the six legs usually has claws at the end. Fast running beetles have long, slender legs. Others have short and stout legs, with flat pads that help them walk on slippery surfaces. Digging beetles have tooth-like projections on their legs to scrape away soil. Most swimming beetles have flat, hind legs.

INTERESTING FACT!

Click beetles make a clicking sound if disturbed. These beetles have a hook-like part that locks the first and second segments of the thorax. When they release the hook, a sudden body jerk produces a clicking sound.

FACT FILE

Smallest: Feather-winged beetles, less than 0.02 inches long.
Largest: the Goliath beetle of Africa grows to about 5.1 inches
Strongest: American burying beetles can lift 200 times their own weight
Hottest: Bombardier beetles can shoot a hot, smelly liquid, 212° F in temperature, from their abdomen

■ Scarab beetles such as dung beetles and tumblebugs feed on dung. They roll the dung into balls and bury it in soil. Females lay one egg in the ball of dung. Some Scarab, like June beetles and Japanese beetles, eat crops

Mixed bag

Many beetles feed on crops, trees or stored food, causing a lot of damage. Such bugs are called pests. However, some beetles are helpful to people. For example, ladybirds and certain other beetles save crops by eating bugs such as aphids. Other beetles, like the dung beetle, are important because they eat dead plants and animals, clearing the environment.

■ Darkling beetles feed on plants and like to walk around. But when disturbed, they assume a head-down and tail-up position. If handled roughly, they emit a dark-coloured, foul-smelling fluid. This behaviour is enough to ward off most predators

Enemy protection

Beetles have many enemies, including birds, reptiles and other bugs. Most beetles protect themselves by biting, hiding or flying away. Some beetles produce a bad smell that puts off predators.

Ballet Dancers

Not all bugs are short, round and ugly. Butterflies, dragonflies and mayflies are very pretty. They have four lacy wings and a slim and long tail that trails behind them. The wings shimmer and gleam in the sunlight when the insect flies. These bugs looks so graceful while flying that they are sometimes referred to as the 'ballet dancers' of the bug world!

Nymph's tale

Young mayflies are called nymphs or naiads. Mayflies lay their eggs in streams and ponds. The nymphs breathe through gills, feed on water plants and live for a few months to two years. They shed their skin when they leave the water, and become winged subimagos, or subadults. Mayflies are the only bugs to go through this stage. After just hours, the subimago becomes a full-grown adult.

■ Mayflies are commonly called dayflies because of their short lives. Adult mayflies live for only a few hours or a few days

■ The dragonfly can hover in mid-air by flapping its wings. It eats other bugs, catching them while flying

Keen eyes

Dragonflies have very good eyesight due to their eye structure. Dragonflies have up to 30,000 facets to their compound eyes; each one is a separate light-sensing organ, or ommatidium, arranged to give nearly 360 degree field of vision.

Masking lip

Dragonfly nymphs remain in the water for one to five years. They have a thick body and a big head and mouth, but no wings. They have a folding lower lip, called a mask, which is half as long as their bodies. The lip has jaw-like hooks at the end and can move out to capture prey.

■ Dobson flies resemble dragonflies. However, they cannot fly as well as dragonflies. Moreover, unlike dragonflies, dobson flies can fold their wings over their backs when not in flight

FACT FILE

Biggest living dragonfly
Megaloprepus coerulatus; wingspan about 7 inches (19 cm)
Smallest
Nannophya pygmaea; 0.59 inches long, wingspan about 0.79 inches
Fastest insect
Capable of 60 mph (97 km/h)

INTERESTING FACT!

Fireflies have a unique form of communication – light! The light organs in a firefly are located on the underside of the abdomen, the last section of an insect's body. A chemical reaction in the light organs produces the firefly's light.

Flying with the wind

The front and back wings of the dragonfly move separately, allowing them to stop and change direction in mid-air. This also helps them to fly at higher speeds. While resting, dragonflies hold their wings open. Their back wings are broader than the front ones.

True Bugs

True bugs occur all over the world. Unlike most other bugs, true bugs have both piercing and sucking mouthparts. These are found in a long, beak-like structure on the body. True bugs mostly feed on plant juices, though some can also suck blood from animals or other bugs.

The young ones of true bugs look like wingless adults. Their metamorphosis does not involve a pupa

Killers by choice

■ Leaf-footed insects, especially their young ones, resemble assassin beetles

A variety of bugs, including caterpillars and cockroaches, often fall prey to 'assassin' bugs. Assassin bugs lie in wait for other bugs and then stab the prey with their beak. The assassin bug injects a toxin that dissolves the prey's tissue. It then sucks up the other bug. Some assassins can produce hissing sounds by rubbing their feeding tube against the underside of their body.

Half wings

True bugs have a kind of "half" wing – with the front wing divided into a leathery hard part and a membranous softer part. These wing covers are held over the back and are often partly folded.

FACT FILE
Number of species
Over 80,000
Length
0.04 inch (1 mm) to 4.3 inches (11 cm)

■ Most cockroaches, like this rainforest cockroach, have wings. However, female cockroaches, nymphs and some species like the Madagascar hissing cockroach do not have wings. Although some winged cockroaches can fly, others are unable to do so

Walking on water

Many true bugs are aquatic. These water striders move on water with their feet barely touching the surface. They detect the ripples of other bugs on the water and run quickly to capture and kill their prey.

Pest problems

Many stink bugs and shield bugs are agricultural pests. They suck plant juices and damage crop production. These bugs are present in large populations. They are also resistant to the sprays that are used to kill such bugs.

■ Some bugs are capable of producing a foul-smelling chemical with the glands on the sides of their bodies. They are known as stink bugs

INTERESTING FACT!

Some true bugs are eaten by humans. A variety of water bug is used in Chinese food. In Thailand, the giant water bug is a delicacy. It is either eaten whole or prepared as sauce for dipping.

Camouflage Specialists

Some bugs, like the leaf and stick bugs, are masters of camouflage – that is, they can blend into their surroundings. It is very difficult to spot these bugs in the forest. This special feature helps bugs to hide from enemies. It also allows them to sneak up quietly on their prey.

Blowing in the wind

In order to completely blend into its surroundings, the leaf insect walks by gently swaying its whole body from side to side. It then looks like a leaf blowing in the wind. This perfect camouflage allows the leaf insect to be active during the day.

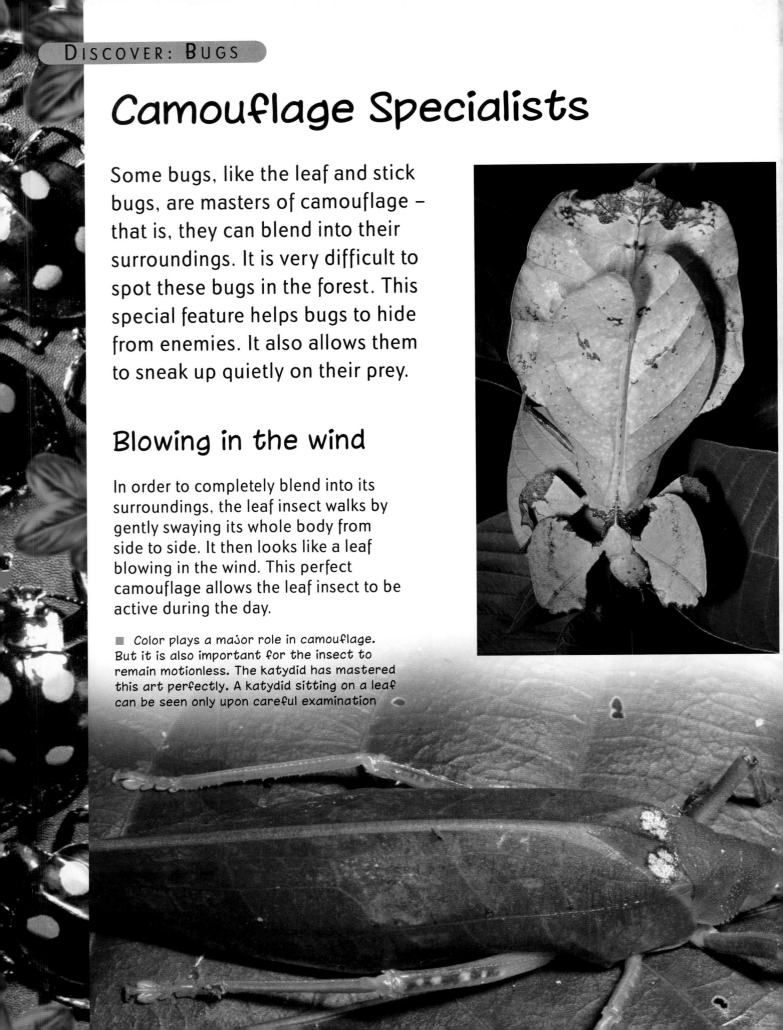

■ Color plays a major role in camouflage. But it is also important for the insect to remain motionless. The katydid has mastered this art perfectly. A katydid sitting on a leaf can be seen only upon careful examination

FACT FILE

Leaf insect
Average length 6 inches
(14 cm); can be as long as
10 inches (25 cm)
Stick insect
Average length 4-6 inches
(10-15 cm);
can be as long as 20 inches
(52 cm)

Hiding in branches

As their names suggest, stick bugs look like branches. You can spot them by looking for a branch that is out of line or attached to the outside edges of leaves. Stick bugs are usually drab in color, but one type of stick bug has a stunning sky-blue color.

■ Certain types of stick bugs have projections along the body, which look like the thorns of a plant

Under leaves

Leaf bugs hang from the underside of tree leaves. At first they look like dried, dead leaves and are tough to spot. Their color can range from pale green to dark brown, depending on the color of the leaves.

■ Walking stick bugs are small and slow-moving. They feed on plant products

Protection sprays

Some camouflage bugs also have other defense mechanisms to deter the enemy. The peppermint stick bug sprays an irritating fluid at its predators, the smell of which is much like a peppermint. The spray can also be foul-smelling.

INTERESTING FACT!
Some leaf bugs have broad-ribbed wings that fold over the back in the shape of a leaf. These bugs can also have enlarged, leaf-like growths on the joint of their legs, giving them their particular name.

Garden Party

Domestic gardens are a fantastic place to observe insects. Among the bugs that can be found in a garden are grasshoppers, crickets and cicadas. These garden bugs are either green or brown in color. They feed on plant products and the remains of other bugs.

Hopping and walking

Grasshoppers can hop, walk and fly. The long legs at the back are used for hopping and the bug can leap about 20 times the length of its body. The shorter front legs are used to hold prey as well as to walk.

■ The cicada is a large-bodied, dark-coloured flying insect. When at rest, it holds the wings over the body like a tent. Male cicadas are the noisiest insects in the world

■ Most grasshoppers are green, olive green or brown in color. But rainbow grasshoppers are very colorful

Eyeing around

A grasshopper has five eyes. Each side of the head has a large compound eye with thousands of single lenses. These eyes allow the bug to see all around. A grasshopper also has three small single eyes. One is above the base of the antenna, one below and one midway between the two antennae. No one knows what function these small eyes have.

INTERESTING FACT!

Certain species of cicadas, called periodical cicadas, take 13-17 years to develop. Depending upon the species, the nymphs spend about 13-17 years underground before coming out to mate. The adult cicadas die soon after mating!

■ The Jerusalem cricket can be found in moist areas in deserts. Because of its surprisingly human-like head it is called 'child of the earth' in some places

■ Grasshoppers are eaten as a delicacy in many countries. They are a good source of protein. Many countries also instruct army men to eat grasshoppers when they get lost and run out of food

Song of love

Male crickets are said to 'sing' songs. And each kind of cricket has a different song. Some trill, while others make a series of chirps. Crickets produce a musical chirping sound by rubbing their two front wings together. It is this sound that leads female crickets to the male!

Cricket info

Crickets are related to grasshoppers but have many differences. The wings of most crickets lie flat over each other on top of their backs. Other crickets only have tiny wings, or are wingless. The slender antennae are much longer than the body in most of these bugs.

Venom and Stings

An insect bite, or a sting, can be very painful and poisonous. A bug uses its bite or sting for two purposes. The first is for protection from enemies. A bite can put off any enemy or even paralyze it. The other use is to get food. Bugs that feed on other bugs use this tactic.

Bee sting

Most bees depend on their stingers, or stings for defending their homes. The sting of a worker bee is straight, with hooks on it. When the bee thrusts the sting into the flesh, the hook holds tight and the stinger pulls out of the bee's body. Glands attached to the sting produce a poison, which is pumped in.

■ Scorpions perform dance-like movements while mating

Death of the worker

Queen bees have a smooth, curved sting that is used to kill other queens. Queens do not lose their stings like worker bees. A worker bee dies soon after losing its sting. Drones have no sting.

■ The earwig gets its name from the belief that it crawls into the ears of humans and lays eggs in their brains! However, this is not true. Earwigs are harmless to humans. But if carelessly handled, the insect can give you a painful pinch with its pincers!

Spider venom

Almost all spiders have venom, which they inject into their victims to paralyze them. But very few spiders are actually venomous enough to cause injury to humans. Some of the commonly found venomous spiders that are harmful to humans include black widow, brown recluse and yellow sac spiders. Although the venom of a black widow is considered highly toxic, hardly any deaths have ever been reported. The bite can, however, be painful and may cause severe adverse reactions.

Venom kills

Scorpions and centipedes are among the most poisonous creatures on earth. They can kill humans and big animals. Both are often mistaken for bugs, although they do not belong to this family.

INTERESTING FACT!
Killer bees are very dangerous. If their hive is disturbed, they attack anything in the surrounding area. They attack in large numbers and their stings can kill people.

House Creatures

You may not like them a lot, but bugs can feel very much at home in your house! The warm conditions and a multitude of ideal hiding spots, as well as plentiful food supplies, make the domestic home an attractive domain.

Dinner time

Female mosquitoes drink blood, while males only sip plant nectar. Houseflies cannot bite or chew, but they can liquefy many solid foods with their saliva. Cockroaches, on the other hand, are scavengers. They will eat a variety of substances, including book binding, paper, soap, plants and dead animals.

INTERESTING FACT!

The buzzing of a fly is actually the sound of its wings beating. A housefly's wings beat about 200 times a second. A mosquito makes more sound, with its wings moving about 1,000 times a second.

■ Certain kinds of mosquitoes carry germs that cause diseases like encephalitis, malaria and yellow fever. When a mosquito bites your body, it may leave germs behind

■ Termites live on trees and have a long, nose-like snout. They can spray glue from their nose, using it to trap other bugs and kill them

FACT FILE

Housefly
Up to 0.24-0.35 inches (6-9 mm) long; wingspan 0.51-0.60 inches (13-15 mm)
Can fly at 4.3 mph (7 kph)

Mosquito
Average length 0.12-0.24 inches (3-6 mm); can fly at 0.99-1.49 mph (1.6-2.4 kph)

Cockroach
Can run up to 3 mph (5 kph)

■ The housefly is often a carrier of diseases such as typhoid fever, cholera, dysentery and anthrax

Flying colors

Flies can have dull-black, brown, gray, or yellowish bodies, covered with fine hair. A few kinds, including soldier flies and hover flies, may have bright orange, white or yellow markings. Some others, such as bluebottles and greenbottles, are shiny blue or green.

Brown and crawly

Cockroaches have flat, oval bodies. Their long legs are covered with bristles that help them to feel. Cockroaches are fast-runners and many of them can fly as well. These bugs have long antennae with organs that can detect certain smells.

■ A cockroach can hold its breath for 40 minutes. Bizarrely, if its head is removed, a cockroach goes on living for up to a week

Keeping them away

The best way to keep bugs away is to keep the house clean. It is advisable not to keep old newspapers or have dirty water stagnate. Any crack in the wall should be sealed, as young cockroaches can crawl into gaps only 0.02 inches (0.5 mm) wide. One can also use sprays. Mosquitoes and cockroaches are tough survivors, though.

Bugs That Harm

Very few insect species are harmful to humans. Less than one per cent of all bugs are really dangerous. But these few bugs can create a lot of havoc. They eat up crops, invade houses and do not spare clothes and furniture either. They can also infect livestock and humans with diseases.

■ Ticks, like fleas, are tiny, bloodsucking animals that live on other animals and humans. But unlike fleas, ticks are not insects. They are, in fact, related to spiders

Crop-eaters

Bugs attack almost all types of plants. The major pests include Hessian flies, which attack wheat; boll weevils, which eat up cotton crops; and corn earworms and chinch bugs, which destroy corn and other crops. Colorado beetles feed on potatoes. Bugs like locusts attack in swarms and can eat up an entire crop field in minutes.

Life-threatening

Houseflies and blowflies carry germs and deposit these in our food or water. They cause diseases like typhoid fever, cholera and dysentery. Insect bites can also cause deadly illnesses like dengue fever, encephalitis, malaria, African sleeping sickness and bubonic plague. Some bugs like fleas and lice live on human bodies and suck our blood.

Home invaders

Bugs create a mess in homes. Cloth moths and carpet beetles make holes in clothes, sofas and carpets. Silverfish can damage books, while termites will burrow into anything made of wood. Ants and cockroaches spoil food and can also transport germs.

■ Mites are smaller versions of ticks and largely live on decaying matter. But some live on humans and animals. The young ones of this red velvet mite live on grasshoppers and locusts, while the adults prey on termites

Kill them fast!

The easiest way to kill a harmful bug is to swat it the minute you see one! But it is not always safe, especially if bugs are in large numbers. The other option is to use special sprays called insecticides, which kill the pests.

■ Many beetles have been found to be harmful to crops. The rhinoceros beetle is a common pest in the tropical regions. It bores into the trunks and leaves of coconut trees and feeds on the tender tissues

■ The praying mantis is often mistaken for a pest. The contrary is true, however; it feeds on other insects, especially crop-eating pests

Bugs That Help

Some bugs can be very helpful for humans. They help in pollination, make products such as honey, feed on harmful bugs, and serve as food for birds and other animals.

Cleaning agents

Bugs help to keep the landscape clean by feeding on animal wastes and dead animals, and also on the remains of dead plants. Bugs that live in the ground enrich the soil with their waste products and dead bodies.

■ Dung beetles eat dung. They either make a ball out of it, or simply dig burrows under or near the food. This eating habit of the dung beetle not only reduces the piles of manure but also improves the quality of soil and helps to control pests and flies

Sweet honey

Honeybees suck up nectar from flowers and store it in their honey stomachs. They return to the hive and spit the nectar back into it. The worker bees in the hive then add enzymes to the nectar. As the water in the nectar evaporates, the nectar changes into honey!

■ Honeybees communicate by dancing. The dance tells worker bees where to find nectar

■ The ladybug eats several kinds of crop-destroying bugs

FACT FILE

Honeybees must tap some 2 million flowers to make 1.1 pounds of honey
They fly over 55,000 miles (88,514 km) for 1.1 pounds of honey
Honeybee flies 15 mph (24 kph); visits 50 to 100 flowers in one trip

INTERESTING FACT!

Some helpful bugs act as parasites, living in - or on - the bodies of harmful bugs. For example, some wasps lay their eggs in caterpillars that damage tomato plants. As the young wasps develop, they feed on the caterpillars.

■ Silkworm cocoons are harvested for the production of silk. The cocoons are usually boiled to help unravel the tightly bonded silk and the silkworm is then often eaten as a delicacy

Bagful of products

Bugs provide us with many valuable products. These include honey and beeswax, made by bees; shellac, made from a substance given off by lac bugs; and silk, produced by silkworms.

Spinning silk

A silkworm is not a worm, but the larva of a moth. A silkworm feeds only on mulberry leaves. It spins a cocoon from where raw silk is obtained. The cocoon is made of a single, continuous thread of raw silk, which is 1,000 feet to 3,000 feet long.

Glossary

Adaptability: A living organism's ability to change or be changed to suit its surroundings or environment

Anthrax: An infectious disease found among warm-blooded animals, especially cattle and sheep. It is caused by the bacterium *Bacillus anthracis*

Aphid: A small, soft-bodied insect of the family Aphididae. It has mouthparts used for piercing and sucking plant sap

Camouflage: A bug's natural method of concealing itself from an enemy by appearing to be part of its surroundings

Carrion: A dead or decaying animal

Cholera: A disease of the small intestine caused by the bacteria *vibrio cholerae.* Symptoms include vomiting, upset stomach, muscle cramps and dehydration

Dengue: A type of fever found in the tropics. It is caused by mosquitoes and symptoms include rash headaches and joint pain

Encephalitis: A disease where the patient suffers inflammation of the brain. Symptoms include headache, drowsiness, nausea and fever

Habitat: An environment where an organism lives and multiplies

Larva: The wingless, wormlike form of bugs that hatches from eggs

Lens: A transparent tissue that is found behind the iris in the eye

Malaria: An infectious disease carried by the Anopheles mosquito. Symptoms include fever and shivering

Membrane: A sheer tissue that covers or connects organs or cells in living organisms

Metamorphosis: The total transformation a larva undergoes into its adult stage

Naiad: A plant that grows underwater. It has narrow leaves and small flowers

Pheromone: A chemical substance that an organism gives out, as a reaction to others of the same species

Pollination: The process by which pollen is transferred to help a plant reproduce

Predator: An animal that preys on other animals for its food

Pupa: The stage of development of an insect between its larva and adult phases

Species: A group of organisms that have identical traits and can interbreed

Spinneret: Special organ situated under the abdomen of spiders, used to spin webs

Yellow fever: Infectious disease caused by a virus carried by the Aedes mosquito. Symptoms include fever, muscle cramps, headache and backache

Index